Teacher Take-Out 3
for Preschoolers

12 Complete Lessons for Teachers on the Go!

Created by **M**elinda **M**ahand

Broadman & Holman grants the buyer permission
to reproduce the activity pages contained within for classroom use only.
Any other use requires written permission from Broadman & Holman.

ISBN 0805402438

©1998 Broadman & Holman Supplies, Nashville, TN, printed in USA.

The Men Who Climbed a Mountain

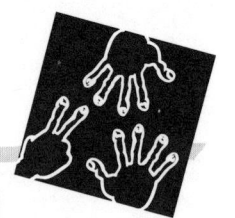

Have you ever been on a mountain? What did you see?

The Bible says Jesus climbed a mountain one day. Up, up, up the mountain climbed Jesus. Jesus climbed up the mountain so He could be alone to think and to pray.

Slowly, the sun started to go down. The moon and the stars came out. It was nighttime, but Jesus didn't care. He stayed on the mountain all night long. Jesus spent the whole night on the mountain, praying to God.

The next morning, Jesus called for His friends.

"Come up here with Me!" called Jesus.

So up, up, up the mountain walked Jesus' friends.

"I need some special helpers," Jesus told His friends. "I have been traveling from town to town helping many people. I have made sick people well. I have taught many people about God. I need some special helpers to work with Me."

So Jesus chose twelve men to be His special helpers.

(As you read the next paragraph, hold up a finger each time you say a helper's name.)

Jesus said: "Simon, I choose you and your brother Andrew to be My helpers. I choose James and his brother John, too. Philip and Bartholomew, Matthew and Thomas, James and Simon, Judas and Judas Iscariot--I choose you twelve to be My special helpers."

From Luke 6:12-16

Bible Song Time
Who Do You Choose?
(tune "Mulberry Bush")

Guide the children to stand in a circle.
Ask one child to walk around the outside of the circle as you sing.
At the end of the song, the child can choose a friend to walk around the circle.
The first child takes the friend's place in the circle.

Who do you choose to be your good friend,
To be your good friend, to be your good friend?
Who do you choose to be your good friend,
At church on Sunday morning?

Bible Fun Time
Come to Me

Ask the girls and boys to stand on one side of the room while you stand on the other side. Comment: "In today's Bible story, we heard that Jesus choose twelve people to come to Him and be His special helpers. In this game, I will choose who can come to me. Listen carefully to hear when to come." Then give instructions such as:

- If you have on red socks, hop to me.
- If you have on a blue dress, tiptoe to me.
- If you have brown eyes, walk backwards to me.
- If your name begins with the letter G, skip to me.

When all the children have come to you, move to another part of the room and begin again.

Who Am I?

Invite a child to pretend to be a helper. The other children may guess which helper the child is pretending to be. You may need to suggest a helper for a child to play out, such as a doctor, a fire fighter, a mail carrier, a cook, a bank teller, a teacher, a waitress, a police officer, a gas station attendant, or a librarian.

Bible Craft Time
Make Helper Coupons

You will need:
- paper
- crayons or washable markers
- stickers (optional)

1st. . . . Cut the paper into large rectangles.

2nd . . . Ask a child to name a way she can help her family, such as pick up toys, make the bed, or give a hug. Print the child's answer on the coupon.

3rd. . . Encourage the child to decorate the coupon using crayons, markers, or stickers.

The Men Who Climbed a Mountain
Activity Sheet

Circle the 12 special helpers that Jesus chose. Each helper has a ● on him.

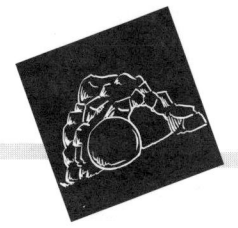 

Tell Everyone He Is Alive!

Have you ever had a really happy day—a day you will always remember? What happened on your happy day?

The Bible tells about a very happy day for a lady named Mary. Let's listen and find out what made Mary so happy.

Long ago, on the very first Easter morning, Mary was walking down the road. It was very early in the morning—so early that it was still very dark outside. But Mary didn't care that it was very dark, because Mary was very sad. She was on her way to the place where Jesus had been buried.

Mary walked to the tomb. She saw the round heavy stone that was the door to the tomb. The door was rolled open. So Mary looked inside the tomb, but Jesus was not there. He was gone! Mary started to cry.

"Why are you crying?" asked a man.

"Because I do not know where Jesus is," answered Mary.

Then the man said, "Mary."

As soon as Mary heard the man say her name, she knew the man was Jesus. Mary was so happy! Jesus was alive!

"Go tell My friends that you have seen Me," Jesus told her.

Mary ran to find Jesus' friends.

"Jesus is alive! I have seen Him!" she said.

From John 20:1-18

Bible Song Time
It's Easter Day
(tune "Michael Row Your Boat Ashore")

Clap your hands, it's Easter day. Hallelujah!
Clap your hands, it's Easter day. Hallelujah!

Tap your toes, it's Easter day. Hallelujah!
Tap your toes, it's Easter day. Hallelujah!

Wave your arms, it's Easter day. Hallelujah!
Wave your arms, it's Easter day. Hallelujah!

Smile and sing, it's Easter day. Hallelujah!
Smile and sing, it's Easter day. Hallelujah!

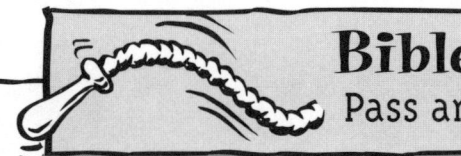

Bible Fun Time
Pass an Easter Surprise

Sit on the floor in a circle. Say: "I will whisper an Easter surprise to the friend next to me. Then we can pass the surprise around the circle."

To the child beside you, whisper, "Jesus is alive." Encourage the child to whisper those words to the next child. Continue whispering all the way around the circle. Ask the last child to whisper the words to you. Then ask the group, "What was our Easter surprise?" The whole group may answer aloud, "Jesus is alive!"

Other ideas include:
- Pass a hand shake.
- Pass a back rub.
- Pass a hand clap. (Have each child clap one after the other around the circle.)
- Try passing faster and faster.

How Do You Walk?

Stand with the children in a circle. Comment: "In our Bible story today, we heard that Mary walked to the place where Jesus was buried. Mary was very sad." Ask, "How do you walk when you are sad?" Encourage the boys and girls to walk in place. Also ask:
- How do you walk when you are happy?
- How do you walk when you are frightened?
- How do you walk when you are tired?
- How do you walk when you are proud?
- How do you walk when you are mad?

Then say: "Our Bible story also said that Mary ran to tell Jesus' friends that Jesus was alive. How do you run to tell someone about Jesus?" Encourage the boys and girls to run in place.

Bible Craft Time
Make an Easter Sights Tube

1st.... Pour the glue into the bowl. Mix a small amount of water into the glue to thin it.

2nd... Invite a child to lightly paint his paper with the glue.

3rd... Tear the tissue paper into small pieces. Guide the child to place pieces of tissue paper onto the glue.

4th... When the paper dries, form a tube by lapping one edge over the other lengthwise. Place a piece of tape all the way along the seam.

5th... As a child looks through the tube, ask, "What do you see through your tube this happy Easter morning?" Listen to the child's answer. Then say: "On the first Easter morning, Mary saw Jesus. Jesus was alive!"

You will need:
- paper
- glue
- unbreakable bowl
- paintbrushes
- tape
- different colors of tissue paper

Tell Everyone He Is Alive!
Activity Sheet

Cut out the round stone.
Cut slit along dotted line.
Insert the stone away from the door.
Color the flowers.
Draw a sun in the sky

Tell Everyone He Is Alive!
Activity Sheet

Cut along the dotted lines to separate the pictures.
Glue the pictures onto a piece of paper in the order they happened.

Mother's Day: What Makes a Good Mother?

Do you have a mother? Do you think she is a good mother? What does she do that makes her a good mother?

We can read about a good mother in the Bible. Listen and see if it sounds like your mother.

Long ago, there lived a boy named Lemuel. Lemuel had a mother. He watched his mother carefully. He listened to the things she said. Lemuel's mother taught him many things.

When Lemuel grew up, he became the king. King Lemuel remembered the things his mother taught him. He wrote down some of the things on paper.

The words of King Lemuel are in the Bible. They say:

A good mother is a wonderful thing.

She works hard to take care of her family.

She teaches her children to be kind.

She loves God and obeys Him.

Her children come to her and say, "Thank you for being such a good mother. We love you."

From Proverbs 31:25-30

Bible Song Time
Thank You, God, for Mother
(tune "For He's a Jolly Good Fellow")

Hold hands with the children. Move in a circle as you hold hands and sing.

Thank You, God, for my mother. Thank You, God, for my mother.

Thank You, God, for my mother. She takes good care of me.

She takes good care of me. She takes good care of me.

Thank You, God, for my mother. She takes good care of me.

Bible Fun Time
Mother, May I?

Ask the preschoolers to stand in a row facing you. In order for the game to move quickly, stand only about five large steps away from the children.

Give an instruction such as, "Take one giant hop." Before moving, the preschoolers ask, "Mother, may I?" You then answer, "Yes, you may." If a child moves before asking, he goes back to the starting line. Other moves include one baby step, two little hops, one tiptoe, one giant step, two skating steps, and three hops on one foot.

The game is over when a child reaches you. Then guide all the children to stand in a row again and start over.

Things Mothers Do

Sit with the children in a circle on the floor. Invite a child to stand up and pretend to do something a mother does. Encourage the other boys and girls to guess what the child is pretending to do. If a child does not have an idea, whisper to him a suggestion of something he can pretend to do. If the preschoolers do not want to pantomime, you can pretend to do the actions and let them guess. Possible actions include:

- ironing
- driving a car
- praying
- brushing hair
- rocking a baby
- mixing something in a bowl
- jogging
- reading
- vacuuming
- buying groceries

Bible Craft Time
Make a Soap Ball Sachet for Mother

 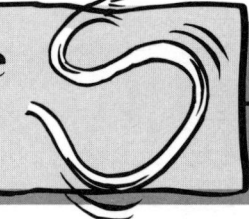

You will need:
- zip-lock bags
- wooden blocks from the preschool room
- bars of soap (motel soaps work well)

1st.... Guide a child to place a piece of soap in a zip-lock bag.

2nd... Invite the child to pound the bag with a wooden block until the soap is finely ground.

3rd... Add small amounts of water until the soap begins to stick together.

4th... Encourage the child to use his hands to mold the soap into balls. One motel soap makes one small soap ball. A full-sized bar of soap makes enough small soap balls for several children.

5th... Place the soap balls on waxed paper to dry. Mothers may use the soap balls as drawer sachets or as soap.

Additional Options:
- Polish the soap balls smooth by rubbing with a pair of clean nylon hose.
- Wrap a soap ball as a gift by placing it in a square of nylon netting. Bring up the four corners and tie the square closed with a piece of ribbon.

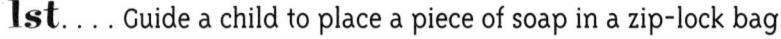

What Makes a Good Mother?
Activity Sheet

Draw your mother's portrait. Color the eyes. Add a nose, a mouth, and hair.

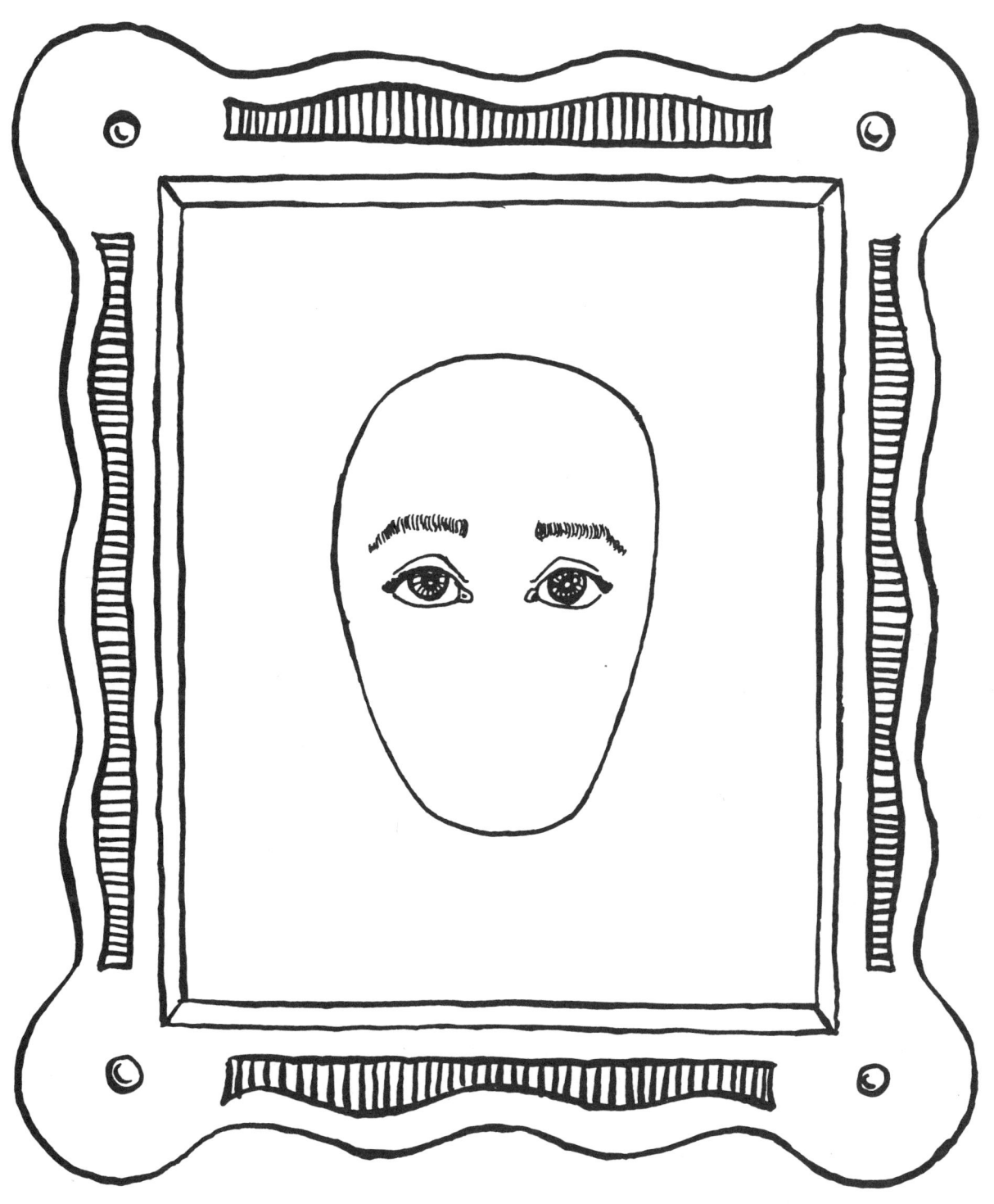

What Makes a Good Mother?
Activity Sheet

Circle the things your mother does.
Find the thing she does best and circle it twice.

Father's Day: What's a Father to Do?

What is your favorite thing to do with your father? (Encourage the girls and boys to tell things they enjoy doing with their fathers. Tell something you like to do with your father, too.)

The Bible tells us about fathers. The Bible tells us that God wants fathers to do something very important for their children. Listen carefully to find out what God wants fathers to do.

Long ago, there lived a man named Abraham. Abraham loved God and obeyed Him. One day God said to Abraham, "You and your wife will have a baby boy next year."

Abraham was very happy. He and his wife had wanted a baby for a long time.

Then God said: "I have chosen Abraham to be a father. I want him to teach his children to obey Me and to do what is right."

The next year, Abraham and his wife had a baby boy, just like God had said. They named the baby boy Isaac.

Abraham was a good father to Isaac. He taught Isaac to do what is right. He taught Isaac to love and obey God.

From Genesis 18:19

Bible Song Time
We Love Daddy
(tune "London Bridge")

When you sing the word "*big*," reach up high.
When you sing the word "*strong*," make muscles with your arms.

Daddy, Daddy, big and strong, big and strong, big and strong.
Daddy, Daddy, big and strong, We love Daddy.

Bible Fun Time
Dress Like Daddy

Locate two sacks. In each sack, place a pair of men's shoes, a cap, and a jacket or shirt. Choose two children to stand several yards in front of the sacks. When you say, "Go," let the children run to the sacks and put on the clothes as fast as they can. The other children can cheer them on. There is no need to declare a "winner." Just let everyone laugh and enjoy the game. When the first two children are through, return the clothes to the sacks and choose two more children to play.

Ball Game

Explain: "Sometimes girls and boys like to play ball with their daddies. Today we will play a ball game with each other." Locate a sponge-type ball, a beanbag, or a wadded piece of paper. Stand with the preschoolers in a circle. Choose one child to stand in the center of the circle.

Throw the ball back and forth across the circle, trying not to let the child in the center catch it. When the child does catch the ball, he goes to the thrower's place in the circle. The thrower then goes to the center of the circle and begins the game again.

Bible Craft Time
Make a "Daddy's Resting" Door Hanger

You will need:
- paper
- scissors
- paper cup
- crayons or washable markers
- glue

1st . . . Print the words "Daddy's Resting" on a piece of paper for each child. Cut out the words.

2nd . . . Invite a child to fold a piece of paper in half lengthwise and then cut along the crease.

3rd . . . Guide the child to set the paper cup near the top edge of one of the rectangles. Trace around the cup.

4th . . . Draw a line from the middle of the top edge of the paper to the circle the child traced.

5th . . . Cut along the line and along the circle to form a door hanger.

6th . . . Encourage the child to glue the words "Daddy's Resting" on the door hanger.

7th . . . Invite the child to decorate the door hanger using crayons or washable markers.

What's a Father to Do?
Activity Sheet

Draw a line from each father to the item that is missing.

What's a Father to Do?
Activity Sheet

Help Daddy drive home.

Jan 7

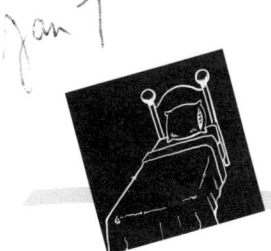 Sleepless Samuel

Have you ever had trouble going to sleep at night? The Bible tells about a boy named Samuel who just couldn't get to sleep. Let's listen and find out what was keeping Samuel awake.

One night long ago, Samuel was lying in bed. Suddenly, Samuel heard someone call his name, "Samuel!"

Samuel jumped up out of bed and ran to the other room. "Here I am," Samuel said to Eli. "I heard you call me."

"I didn't call you," said Eli. "Go back to bed."

So Samuel went to bed again. Then he heard someone call for the second time, "Samuel!"

Samuel jumped up and went back to Eli's room. "Here I am," said Samuel. "I heard you call me."

"I didn't call you," said Eli. "Go back to bed."

So Samuel went back to bed. Then he heard someone call for the third time, "Samuel!"

Samuel jumped up again and went to Eli's room. "Here I am," said Samuel. "I heard you call me."

Then Eli said: "Go back to bed. I didn't call you. God is calling you. If you hear Him call again, say, 'Speak, Lord. I am listening.'"

So Samuel went back to bed. He listened carefully. Soon he heard God call, "Samuel!"

"Speak, Lord. I am listening," answered Samuel.

So God talked to Samuel that night. And from then on, as Samuel grew, God took good care of him.

From 1 Samuel 3:1-10

 Bible Song Time
Jump Up Samuel
(tune "She'll Be Comin' Round the Mountain")

When you sing the words "Jump up," jump up in the air.
When you sing the word "Listen," cup your hands around your ears.

Jump up Samuel when you hear God call to you.
Jump up Samuel when you hear God call to you.
Jump up Samuel when you hear God.
Jump up Samuel when you hear God.
Jump up Samuel when you hear God call to you.

Listen Samuel when you hear God speak to you.
Listen Samuel when you hear God speak to you.
Listen Samuel when you hear God.
Listen Samuel when you hear God.
Listen Samuel when you hear God speak to you.

Bible Fun Time
Musical Stop and Go

Explain: "Each time Samuel heard a voice, he jumped up out of bed. Today we will play a game where we jump up, too."

Encourage the girls and boys to march around the room as you play music on a tape recorder or record player. When you suddenly stop the music, everyone must quickly stop and squat down to the floor. When the music begins again, everyone can jump up and begin marching again.

Billowing Blanket

Bring a blanket from home. Explain: "Our Bible story today said that Samuel was asleep in bed when he heard God talking to him. Let's play a game with a blanket I brought from my bed."

Guide the children to stand around the blanket and hold on to it with both hands. Show the boys and girls how to lift the blanket up over their heads by raising their arms high. When they slowly lower their arms, the blanket will billow slightly. After lifting and lowering several times, say: "The next time we lift the blanket, I want Thomas and Bryce to run under the blanket and trade places." Lift the blanket and encourage the two children to run underneath and trade places. Continue naming two children to trade places until everyone has had a turn.

Expand the game by asking a child to name a friend she wants to trade places with. Give each child a turn to name a friend and trade places.

Bible Craft Time
Make a Finger Puppet of Sleeping Samuel

You will need:
- construction paper
- sharp scissors
- crayons or washable markers

1st . . . . Cut a piece of construction paper into four quarters.

2nd . . . Invite a child to color one of the pieces to look like Samuel's bed. The child may draw a pillow and decorate the blanket portion of the bed.

3rd . . . When the child is finished, use sharp scissors to gently poke a hole in the middle of the paper. Gently enlarge the hole so the child can stick her index finger through it.

4th . . . Guide the child to bend her finger to make Samuel lay down in bed. The child can straighten her finger for Samuel to get up.

Sleepless Samuel
Activity Sheet

Finish the Bible story picture:
Draw the moon shining in Samuel's window.
Draw a flame on Samuel's lamp.
Decorate Samuel's blanket.
Color the picture.

Sleepless Samuel
Activity Sheet

Look at each group of things we use at night.
Draw an X through the item in each group that does not belong.

Who Can Help Naaman?

Have you ever been sick? Who helped you get well? Did your Mommy and Daddy help? Did your doctor help?

The Bible tells about a little girl who helped a sick man named Naaman. The girl lived at Naaman's house. The girl worked for Naaman's wife. Each day when the girl saw Naaman, she felt very sad. Naaman had sore places all over his body. He was very, very sick. "Who can help Naaman?" wondered the girl.

Then one day the girl thought of a way to help. "I will tell Naaman about Elisha," said the girl. "I know Elisha can tell Naaman how to get well."

When Naaman heard about Elisha, he decided to go see him. Strong horses quickly pulled Naaman's chariot down the road. When Naaman came to Elisha's house, he stopped the chariot.

"How can I get well?" Naaman asked Elisha.

"Go to the river," said Elisha. "Wash in the river seven times. Then you will be well."

So Naaman went to the river. He washed in the river seven times. Suddenly, the sores on Naaman's body were gone. Naaman was well!

The little girl must have been very happy and excited when Naaman came home. She had helped Naaman find a way to get well.

From 2 Kings 5:1-16

Encourage the children to play out each action you sing about.
The children may also want to suggest their own helpful actions to sing about.

A helper I will be, A helper I will be,

I will help stir the food,*

A helper I will be.

* Also sing *"wash the car"*, *"feed my dog"*, *"sweep the floor"*,
"water plants", and *"fold the clothes"*.

Bible Fun Time
Circle of Kindness

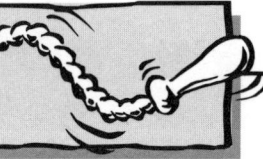

Locate a ball that bounces. Explain: "The little girl who helped Naaman was very kind. Let's play a game where we can be kind, too."

Stand with the preschoolers in a large circle. Invite a child to stand in the center of the circle, holding the ball. Using the child's name, say the rhyme:

"Jason is standing in the ring.

Jason can do a kind thing."

The child may then bounce the ball to a friend. When the friend catches the ball, the friend goes to the center of the circle. Say the rhyme again, using this child's name. Encourage him to bounce the ball to a friend. Continue playing until every child has a turn to bounce the ball.

Bible Craft Time
Make a Helper's Hat

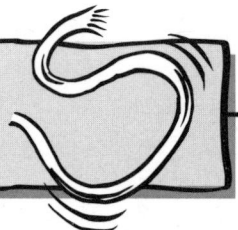

You will need:
- paper plates
- scissors
- crayons or washable markers
- tape or stapler

1st.... Cut a slit in a paper plate from one edge of the plate to the center of the plate.

2nd... Lap one edge over the other to form a cone-shaped hat. Tape or staple at the seam.

3rd... Invite a child to color the hat. The child might choose to color the hat red like a fire fighter's hat or blue like a police officer's hat. The child might color a red cross on the hat to represent a nurse's cap, or he might choose to decorate the helper's hat in his own unique way.

Who Can Help Naaman?
Activity Sheet

Find the hidden items Naaman's helper might have used.

Who Can Help Naaman?
Activity Sheet

Match the helper and the tool.

Sept 24

Daniel: Fit for a King

Can you make a muscle? (Pretend to make a muscle with your arm. Encourage the boys and girls to make muscles also.)

The Bible tells about a king who was looking for some strong, healthy men to work for him. One day, the king said to his helper: "Go find the healthiest and strongest young men in all the land of Israel. Bring the young men to me."

The king's helper looked and looked. Finally, he chose a young man named Daniel and three of Daniel's friends.

The king's helper said, "You will learn how to work for the king."

At mealtime, the helper brought some of the king's food for Daniel and his friends to eat.

Daniel and his friends looked at the food. They knew God did not want them to eat this food. This food was not good for them to eat.

Daniel and his friends had to make a hard choice. They had to decide if they would do what God wanted them to do or if they would do what the king wanted them to do.

Daniel said to the king's helper, "Please let us have vegetables to eat and water to drink."

"No," said the king's helper. "The king will be angry if you do not stay strong and healthy. You must eat this food."

"Please, let my friends and me have vegetables to eat and water to drink for ten days," said Daniel. "After ten days, we will still be strong and healthy. You will see."

"Well, OK, we'll try it," said the helper.

So for ten days, Daniel and his friends ate lots and lots of vegetables. For ten days, they drank lots and lots of water.

After the ten days were over, the kings' helper looked at Daniel and his friends.

"You are healthier than any of the other young men," he said. "I will keep on serving you the food that makes you healthy and strong."

From Daniel 1:1-20

Bible Song Time
What Would You Like?
(tune "Mulberry Bush")

Hold hands with the children in a circle. Invite one child to stand in the center of the circle. As you sing, move in circle around the child. At the end of the song, the child in the center can name his favorite food. Then choose another child to stand in the center, and sing the song again.

What would you like to eat today, to eat today, to eat today?
What would you like to eat today? Tell me, tell me, tell me.

Bible Fun Time
My Groceries

If possible, bring a bag of groceries from home. If you cannot bring groceries, play this game by just thinking of foods to describe.

Look inside your grocery sack and choose a food to describe. For instance, if you choose an apple, say: "I went to the grocery store, and I chose a food that grows on a tree. It is shiny and red. It crunches when you take a bite." Keep describing until a child guesses the correct food. Then take the food out of the grocery sack and show it to the children.

Begin again by describing another food.

Tip: Use foods that are familiar to the preschoolers, such as apple, orange, banana, carrot, crackers, cereal, bread, and popcorn.

Standing for What Is Right

On slips of paper, print several right and wrong choices the girls and boys might make. For instance, some choices might be:

- Share my toys with my sister.
- Obey my mother.
- Put away my toys.
- Fight over a toy.
- Be kind to animals.
- Hit my brother when I'm mad.
- Be mean to my friend.
- Help my father.
- Throw my trash on the floor.
- Tear pages out of a book.

Place the slips of paper in a bag.

Explain: "Daniel did the right thing. He obeyed God. Daniel made the right choice. In this game, we can choose the right thing to do, too."

Sit with the children in a circle on the floor. Place the bag in front of you. Invite a child to choose a paper. Say: "If the paper tells the right thing to do, we will all stand up. If the paper tells the wrong thing to do, we will all sit down."

Read the statement on the paper. If it is the right thing to do, stand up. To the tune "The Farmer in the Dell, sing: "We will all stand up. We will all stand up. We'll do what's right with all our might. We will all stand up."

Each time a right choice is read, stand and sing the song. Each time a wrong choice is read, sit down.

Bible Craft Time
Make a Good Foods Menu

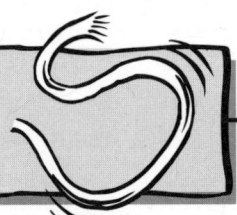

You will need:
- paper
- scissors
- glue
- crayons or washable markers

1st . . . Print the words "Good Food Menu" on a piece of paper for each child.

2nd . . . Print simple prices such as 25 cents, 50 cents, and 75 cents on a piece of paper. Cut out the prices.

3rd . . . Give each child a menu.

4th . . . Invite the children to draw good food choices on their menus. They can also cut food choices out of paper and glue them onto the menu. For instance, small yellow clippings could represent corn. Small green clippings could represent beans. Small orange circles could represent sliced carrots. Brown shapes could represent chicken nuggets.

5th . . . Encourage the girls and boys to glue a price next to each food choice.

Daniel: Fit for a King
Activity Sheet

Draw a line connecting the one food that is in all four columns.
What other matches can you make?

Daniel: Fit for a King
Activity Sheet

Trace each line from the utensil to the food you would eat with that utensil.
Use a different color of crayon to trace each line.

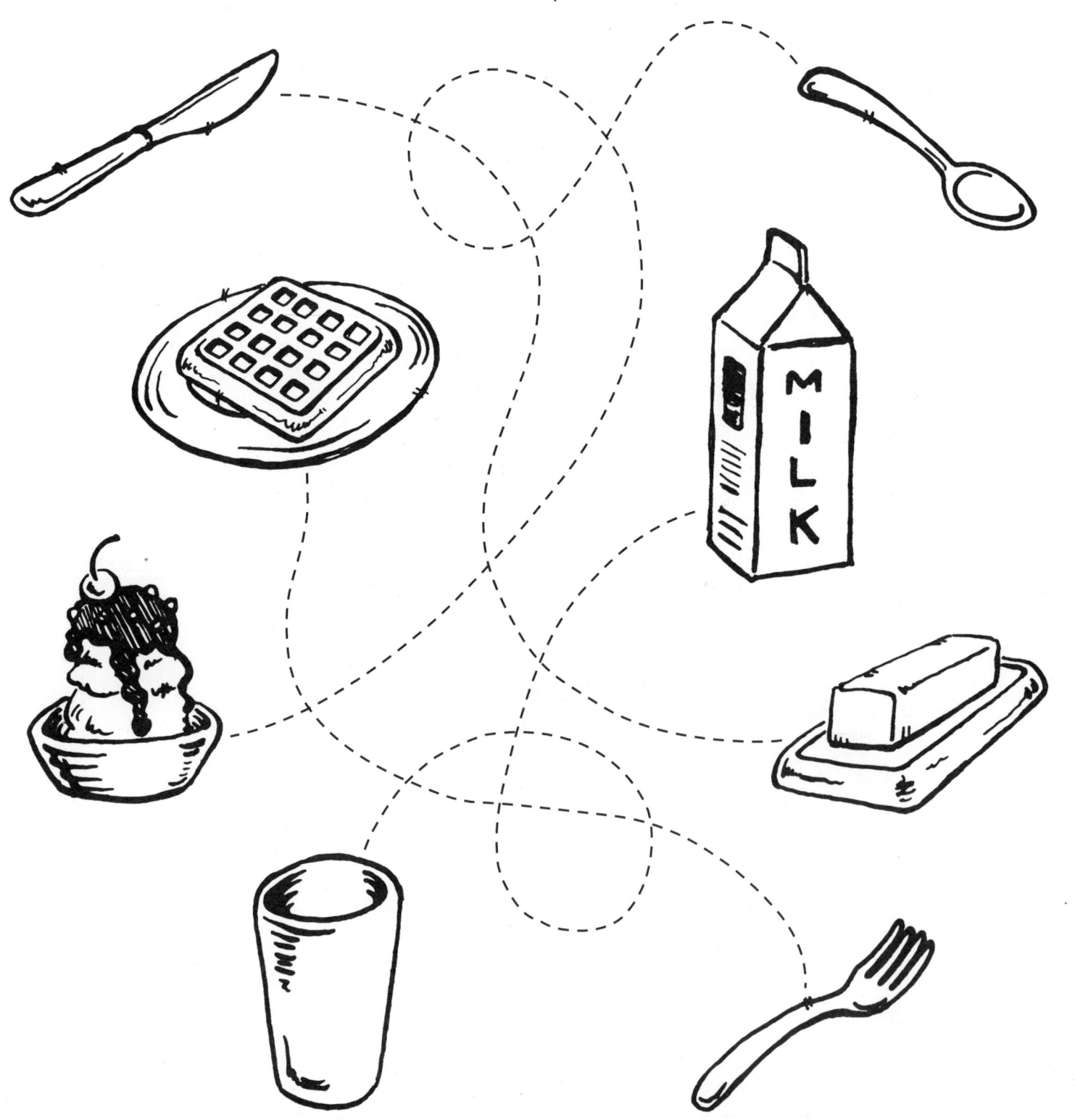

Nov 5

The Man Who Came in Through the Roof

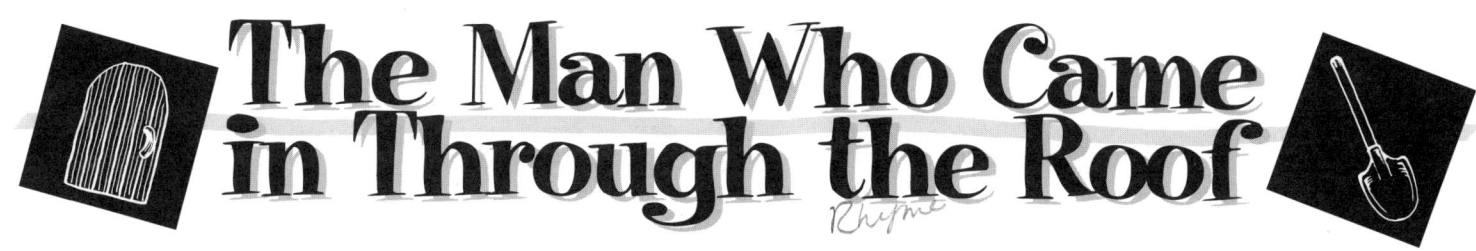

When you go into a house, how do you get inside? Do you go in through a window? Do you go down the chimney? No, you go in through the door!

The Bible tells about a man who went into a house one day. But this man did not go in through the door. Listen carefully to find out how the man got inside.

Long ago there was a man who could not walk. The man's legs did not work. He had to lay down on a pallet all day long.

One day, four of the man's friends were going to see Jesus.

"I wish I could go with you to see Jesus," the man with hurt legs told his friends.

"You can go," said one friend.

"How?" asked the man. "You know I can't walk."

"We will take you," offered his four friends.

Each man lifted a corner of the pallet. They carried their friend to see Jesus.

When the men came to the house where Jesus was, many people were inside. So many people were listening to Jesus that there was no more room in the house. The men could not get inside the door.

"I have an idea," said one of the men. "If we make a hole in the roof, we can lower our friend into the room."

Carefully the men carried their friend up to the roof of the house.

Scrape, scrape, scrape, the men began digging a hole through the mud roof. When the hole was large enough, the men lowered their friend down into the house. Gently, they set him on the ground right in front of Jesus.

Jesus looked at the man and smiled. "Get up. Pick up you pallet, and go to your house," Jesus said.

The man stood up. He picked up his pallet. He could walk! The man was so happy!

All the people watching were amazed. They praised God and said, "We have never seen anything like this before!"

From Mark 2:1-5, 11-12

Bible Song Time
The Leg Action Song
(tune "Row Your Boat")

I can bend my knees, I can bend my knees.
Watch me, and you will see, I can bend my knees!

Also sing, "I can tap my toes", "I can jump up high",
"I can walk in place", and "I can sit back down".

Bible Fun Time
My Friend Can Walk

Stand in a circle with the children. When you call out, "My friend can't walk," all the children squat to the ground. When you call out, "My friend can walk," all the children jump up. Try to fool the children by calling out the phrase quickly or by repeating the same phrase when no one expects it.

Catch the Cane

Locate a cane, a long stick, or a yardstick. Sit with the boys and girls in a circle on the floor. Invite one child to stand in the center of the circle. Guide the child to hold the cane so that one end is resting on the floor.

The child calls out the name of a friend and then lets go of the cane. The friend must catch the cane before it hits the floor. If the friend does not catch the cane, the friend goes to the center of the circle and holds the cane. If the friend does catch the cane, the first child calls another name.

Bible Craft Time
Make a String Painting

You will need:
- paper
- yarn
- scissors
- two colors of liquid tempera paint
- two spoons
- two plastic bowls

1st.... Pour a different color of paint into each plastic bowl.

2nd... Cut lengths of yarn.

3rd... Use a spoon to poke a strand of yarn into each bowl of paint. Leave one end of each strand of yarn out of the bowl.

4th... Invite a child to pull the yarn out of each bowl of paint. Lay the yarn strands on a piece of paper.

5th... Fold the paper on top of the yarn strands. Encourage the child to press and rub on the paper.

6th... Pull the yarn strands out of the paper.

7th... Unfold the paper to see the pretty design.

8th... Comment: "The yarn strands remind me of long ropes. The four men in our Bible story today used long ropes to lower their friend into the house where Jesus was."

The Man Who Came in Through the Roof
Activity Sheet

Draw ropes from the friends' hands to the pallet.
Color the Bible story picture.

The Man Who Came in Through the Roof
Activity Sheet

Circle the people who are using their legs.

Oct. 2

The Man Without a Friend

Do you have a friend? (Go around the circle asking each child to name one friend. If a child cannot name a friend, suggest the child who is sitting next to him, or say, "I will be your friend.")

The Bible tells about a man named Zacchaeus who didn't have any friends--not even one! Zacchaeus didn't have any friends because he was mean to people. He cheated people and took their money.

One day Jesus came to the town where Zacchaeus lived. Zacchaeus wanted to see Jesus. Zacchaeus had heard that Jesus loved everyone. "I wonder if Jesus will love me," thought Zacchaeus.

Many people were crowding beside the road. "Jesus must be over there," thought Zacchaeus. He looked, but he could not see Jesus. He stood on tiptoe. He still could not see Jesus.

Zacchaeus decided to climb a sycamore tree beside the road. When Jesus came down the road, Zacchaeus would be able to see Him.

Zacchaeus climbed up into the tree. Soon he saw Jesus coming. When Jesus came to the sycamore tree, He stopped. He looked up at Zacchaeus.

Then Jesus said: "Zacchaeus, come down. I'm going to your house today." Zacchaeus climbed down out of the tree. He was so excited!

Zacchaeus took Jesus home with him. Jesus told Zacchaeus that God loved him. Then Zacchaeus said: "Jesus, I will give half my money to poor people. I will give back all the money I've taken from others."

Jesus smiled at Zacchaeus. Zacchaeus knew that now he finally had a friend.

From Luke 19:1-10

Bible Song Time
Two Friends
(tune "For He's a Jolly Good Fellow")

Zacchaeus climbed up a tall tree. (Pretend to climb.)
Zacchaeus climbed up a tall tree. Zacchaeus climbed up a tall tree,
To try to see Jesus. To try to see Jesus,
(Cup hands around eyes as if trying to see better.)
To try to see Jesus. Zacchaeus climbed up a tall tree, to try to see Jesus.

Then Jesus walked up to the tree. (Walk in place.)
Then Jesus walked up to the tree. Then Jesus walked up to the tree,
And said, "Zacchaeus, come down." And said, "Zacchaeus, come down."
(Wave arm down as if signaling someone to come down.) *And said, "Zacchaeus, come down."*
Then Jesus walked up to the tree, And said, "Zacchaeus, come down."

They ate their dinner together. (Pretend to eat.)
They ate their dinner together. They ate their dinner together,
Because they were good friends. Because they were good friends.
(Shake hands with a friend beside you.) *Because they were good friends.*
They ate their dinner together, Because they were good friends.

Bible Fun Time
Let's Go for a Walk

Explain: "Jesus was walking down the street when He saw Zacchaeus in the tree. Let's pretend we are walking down the street, too." Encourage the boys and girls to walk in place. Then ask:
- "How would you walk if you were in sticky mud?"
- "How would you walk if you were big and strong?"
- "How would you walk if you were on ice?"
- "How would you walk if you were on hot, hot sand?"
- "How would you walk through the water in a swimming pool?"
- "How would you walk if you were barefoot on a rocky driveway?"
- "How would you walk if you were on soft, thick carpet?"
- "How would you walk if you were in a parade?"

This Is My Friend

Explain: "Jesus was a friend to Zacchaeus. Today we will play a game where we are friends to each other."

Stand with the children in a circle, holding hands. Raise the arm of the child on your right and say, "This is my friend (say the child's name)." That child then raises the arm of the child to her right and says, "This is my friend." Continue around the circle until each child has been introduced.

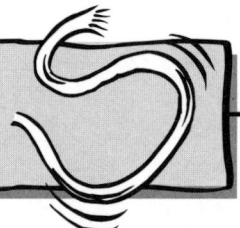

Bible Craft Time
Make a Leaf Screen

You will need:
- leaves
- waxed paper
- scissors
- yarn
- hole punch
- an old towel
- iron
- extension cord

1st . . . . Give a child a piece of waxed paper. Invite the child to arrange several leaves on the paper.

2nd . . . Place a piece of waxed paper on top of the leaves.

3rd . . . Cover your ironing surface with an old towel. Place the child's paper on the towel. Iron the paper until the two waxed sheets stick together.
Note: An adult must be with the iron at all times. Keep the iron out of preschoolers' reach.

4th . . . Encourage the child to trim the paper so the edges are even.

5th . . . Punch two holes in the top of the paper.

6th . . . Thread a strand of yarn through the holes so the paper will hang on a window latch.

The Man Without a Friend
Activity Sheet

Match each shadow to its shape in the Bible story picture.

The Man Without a Friend

Activity Sheet

Draw a line from the tree to each item that belongs in the tree.

The Voice of Thunder

Have you ever listened to thunder during a rainstorm? What did it sound like?

The Bible tells about some people who heard thunder, but there wasn't a rainstorm. What was making the thunder? Listen carefully to find out.

Moses and the people were traveling. They had walked and walked for many days. One day they came to a tall mountain. The mountain was called Mount Sinai. Moses and the people stopped and camped at the bottom of Mount Sinai.

Then Moses decided to climb the mountain. Up, up, up Mount Sinai climbed Moses.

Suddenly he heard someone talking to him. The voice sounded like thunder. The people camping at the bottom of the mountain heard the voice, too. They saw lightning and heard thunder. The thunder was the voice of God. God was talking to Moses on Mount Sinai.

God said: "I have taken good care of you and the people. Now I will give you some rules."

So God wrote down ten rules. He wrote them on tablets made of stone. When God was finished, He gave the tablets to Moses.

Then Moses walked back down the mountain and talked to the people.

"We saw the lightning and heard the thunder," said the people.

"Do not be afraid," said Moses. "The thunder was God's voice. God has given us ten rules to help us know how to love Him and how to love each other."

From Exodus 20:1-17; 32:15-16

Bible Song Time
Ten Rules
(tune "Happy Birthday")

Hold up a finger each time you sing a number until all ten fingers are up.
Sing the song several times.
The last time you sing, change the last line to say,
"Now we'll let the song end."

One, two, three, four, five, six,
Seven, eight, nine, and ten.
God gave ten rules to Moses.
Now we'll sing it again.

Bible Fun Time
Lightning and Thunder

Explain: "The people saw the lightning and heard the thunder while God talked to Moses. First, they saw the lightning. Then they heard the thunder. Thunder is the sound that comes after the lightning."

Guide the children to form two rows and stand several yards apart, facing each other. One row of children is the lightning, and one row is the thunder. When you say, "Lightning," the lightning row strikes and moves like lightning. The other row responds by booming like thunder. After several strikes, reverse roles.

Moses Says

Guide the boys and girls to stand in a row. Explain: "Moses told the people about the rules God had written. The people listened carefully to everything Moses said. Today we will listen carefully while we play the game 'Moses Says.' Listen carefully to what I say. I will tell you something to do, such as, 'Moses says, "Touch your toes."' Then you can do what I said. But if I just say, 'Touch your toes,' don't do it. Wait till I say, 'Moses says, "Touch your toes."'"

Give instructions such as:
- "Moses says, 'Wiggle your nose.'"
- "Moses says, 'Reach up high.'"
- "Moses says, 'Turn around.'"
- "Moses says, 'Shake your head.'"
- "Moses says, 'Wave your arms.'"
- "Moses says, 'Jump up and down.'"

Every once in awhile, give an instruction without saying, "Moses says." For instance, say, "Clap your hands." If the child does the action anyway, just laugh and begin again.

Bible Craft Time
Make a Clay Tablet

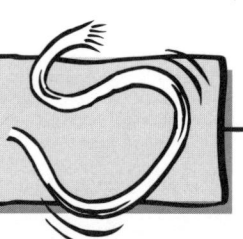

You will need:
- 4 cups flour
- 1 cup salt
- 1 cup cool water
- mixing bowl
- spoon
- craft sticks

1st.... Mix the flour, salt, and water in a bowl. Knead well.

2nd... Give each child a small piece of clay. Encourage the child to pat the clay until it is flat.

3rd... Invite a child to use a craft stick to make marks on the clay "tablet."

4th... Comment, "God wrote the ten commandments on tablets made out of rock."

5th... The children can take their tablets home. The tablet will harden as it dries.

The Voice of Thunder
Activity Sheet

Connect the dots to discover what the Ten Commandments were written on.

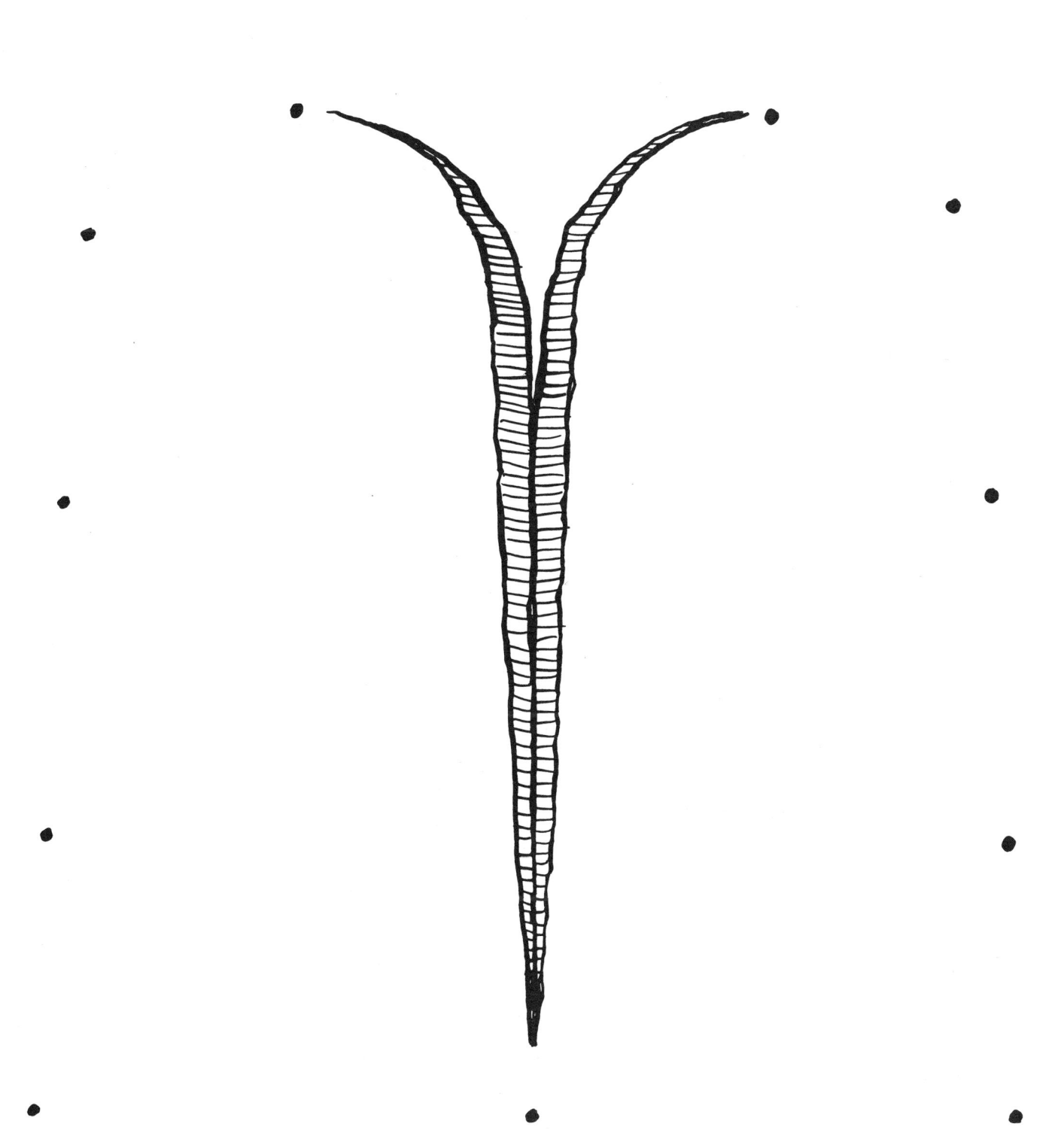

The Voice of Thunder
Activity Sheet

Cut out the strip of faces. Then snip the faces apart. Glue the smiling faces to the pictures of children who are doing what God would want them to do. Glue the frowning faces to the pictures of children who are not doing what God would want them to do.

The Quiet Coins

Have you ever been in a church service when they passed the offering plate? Did your parents let you put in some money? What do you think our offering money buys? (Briefly talk to the children about offering money that pays for Bibles, church buildings, and missionaries.)

The Bible tells about a time when Jesus saw a woman give a very special offering. Let's listen and find out why it was so special.

Clink, clink, clink. Jesus heard the people giving their money at church. Clink, clink. The people dropped their money into the offering box. When a rich person gave a big offering, the money made a lot of noise. Then everyone would look to see who had given such a big offering.

After a while, Jesus saw a very poor woman walk up to the offering box. The poor woman dropped two small coins into the box. The coins were so small that they did not make a big sound. The people did not notice the woman's offering. But Jesus noticed.

"Look at this woman," Jesus told His helpers. "She has given a very special offering. The rich people gave only their extra money. This poor woman gave all the money she had."

From Mark 12:41-44

Bible Song Time
The Offering
(tune "She'll Be Comin' Round the Mountain")

The poor woman gave God everything she had. (Clap your hands.)
The poor woman gave God everything she had.
Two small coins were all she had, (Hold up two fingers.)
But her gift made Jesus glad. (Give a great big smile.)
The poor woman gave God everything she had.

Bible Fun Time
Offering Plate Pass

Borrow an offering plate from the sanctuary or locate a basket that can be used as an offering plate. Prepare a cassette tape player or a record player to play music during the game.

Ask the girls and boys to sit on the floor. Say: "The Bible story told about a woman who gave an offering at church. At our church, we pass an offering plate so people can give money. Today we will pass the offering plate while the music plays. When the music stops, whoever has the offering plate can stand up."

Play the music and pass the offering plate. After it has gone around the circle once or twice, stop the music. When a child stands up with the plate, invite the child to start and stop the music as the game begins again.

Optional: If you make the offering envelopes described below, you can use the envelopes as part of this game. Each time a child is holding the offering plate when the music stops, give the child a penny. The child can place the penny in the offering envelope he made. Make sure the music stops on each child several times.

What Did You Bring?

Explain: "The woman in today's Bible story brought an offering to church. Let's play a game about things we brought to church today." Give the following instructions. Allow time after each instruction for the preschoolers to do the action.

If you brought two hands, clap them together.
If you brought two toes, tap them on the floor.
If you brought your head, nod it up and down.
If you brought your voice, let out a big roar.

If you brought two ears, give them a little tug.
If you brought two legs, turn round and round.
If you brought your smile, show it to me right now.
If you brought two knees, bend them up and down.

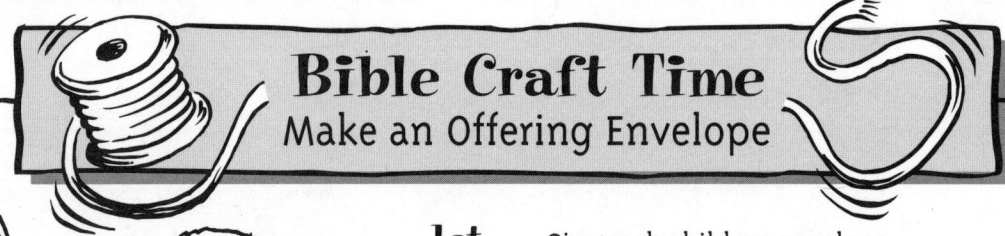

If you brought two feet, march like a soldier.
If you brought two eyes, look up to the sky.
If you brought your nose, give it a wiggle.
If you brought two arms, stretch them up real high.

Bible Craft Time
Make an Offering Envelope

You will need:
- envelopes
- crayons or washable markers
- pennies (optional)

1st . . . . Give each child an envelope.

2nd . . . Invite the children to decorate their envelopes.

3rd . . . Say: "When we give an offering at church, we put the money in an envelope."

4th . . . Give each child a few pennies to put in his envelope, or give each child pennies as you play the game "Offering Plate Pass," described above. Encourage the children to place their envelopes in the offering plate the next time they attend a worship service.

If you did not bring pennies for this activity, encourage the children to take their envelopes home. When a child saves some coins to put in the envelope, he can bring it to church and place it in the offering plate.

The Quiet Coins
Activity Sheet

Find 10 hidden coins.

The Quiet Coins
Activity Sheet

Draw a line from the church to each item your offering money buys.

Too Many Animals!

Do you have a pet at your house? What kind of pet is it? What do you do to take care of your pet?

The Bible says that long ago there lived a man named Abram. Abram didn't have just one pet. Abram had many animals. He had sheep and goats. He had camels and oxen. Abram had helpers to take care of his animals, too.

In the same area, there lived a man named Lot. Lot was Abram's nephew. Lot had many animals, just like his Uncle Abram. Lot had many helpers to take care of his animals, too.

Each morning Abram's helpers led his animals out to the field to eat grass and drink water. Each morning Lot's helpers led his animals out to eat grass and drink water, too.

One morning Abram's helpers began to fuss with Lot's helpers: "Take your animals to another field for grass and water. This field is for Abram's animals."

Lot's helpers said, "No! We will not leave. This field is for Lot's animals."

Abram heard the helpers fussing. He told Lot: "I'm sorry our helpers are fussing. I want our helpers to be friendly."

Abram looked around at all the animals. "We have too many animals to use the same field," said Abram. "Why don't we each move to a different place? You choose the land you want, and I will take the rest."

Lot looked at the land that was grassy and near the river. "That is the land I want," said Lot.

So Lot and his family moved to the grassy land near the river.

Abram looked at the land that was left. "I will take the land that Lot did not want," said Abram.

So Abram and his family moved to the hills. Then both men had plenty of grass and water for their animals, and their helpers never fought again.

From Genesis 13:1-18

Bible Song Time
Abram's Song
(tune "Are You Sleeping?")

A teacher can sing the first phrase of each line and the children can echo it back, or everyone can sing the whole song together.

Are you hungry, are you hungry,
Little sheep, Little sheep?
My helpers will find you, my helpers will find you,
Food to eat, food to eat.

Are you thirsty, are you thirsty,
Little cow, little cow?
My helpers will find you, my helpers will find you,
Water now, water now.

Bible Fun Time
Animal Match

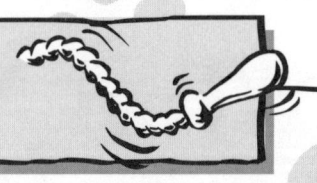

Explain: "Abram and Lot had many, many animals. They both needed good land so their animals would have grass to eat and water to drink. Today we will play a game where we pretend to be animals."

Go around the room whispering the name of an animal in each child's ear. Whisper each animal name to two or three children. When you say, "Go," the girls and boys start making their animal's sound and start moving around the room like their animal. When children with the same animal find each other, they sit down together. When all the children are seated, whisper new animals and begin again.

Tip: Use animals the preschoolers can easily imitate, such as a dog, a cat, a frog, a cow, a sheep, and a lion.

Animal Action

Stand in a circle with the boys and girls. Say: "I am going to tell you something that an animal does. If what I say is true, you can copy me. If what I say is not true, don't copy me."

Then hop up and down and say, "Rabbits hop." Encourage the children to hop up and down with you. Then give several other true statements. For instance:

- Say, "Dogs bark, woof, woof."
- Flap your arms and say, "Birds fly."
- Bend from the waist and clasp your hands together like an elephant's trunk. Say, "Elephants swing their trunks."
- Say, "Cats purr, purr, purr."
- Squat on the floor like a frog. Say, "Frogs jump." Then jump up like a frog.
- Stretch up high and say, "Giraffes reach up high."

Every once in awhile, choose something that isn't true, such as flapping your arms and saying, "Lions fly." If anyone imitates you, just laugh and say: "Lions don't fly! What do lions do? Lions roar. ROAR!"

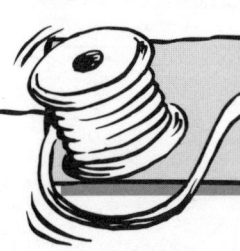

Bible Craft Time
Share an Apple Dumpling Snack

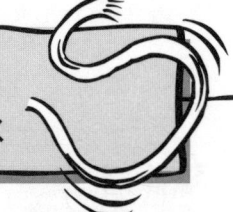

You will need:
- sugar cookies
- applesauce
- grated cheddar cheese
- plastic spoons
- paper plates
- optional: a toaster oven, small baking sheet, oven mitt, and spatula

1st.... Place a sign on the door that says: "Parents, we will be tasting sugar cookies, applesauce, and cheddar cheese. Is your child allergic?" Place a similar sign on the door of the class you plan to share your snack with.

2nd... Give a child a sugar cookie.

3rd.... Guide the child to spread a spoonful of applesauce on top of the cookie.

4th... Invite the child to sprinkle cheddar cheese on top of the applesauce.

5th... You may warm the apple dumpling snack in a toaster oven or may eat it without warming. It is delicious either way!

6th... Also make enough apple dumpling snacks to share with the children in another preschool class. Remark: "Abram was kind. He shared the land with Lot. He let Lot choose some land to live on. Then Abram took the land that was left. We can be kind, too. We can share our apple dumpling snacks with another class. We will eat the snacks that are left."

Too Many Animals!
Activity Sheet

Find 5 ways the Bible story pictures are different.

Too Many Animals!
Activity Sheet

Look at the animals in the field.
Can you help the mother animals find their babies?